Experimenting with Nature Study

Alan Ward

Illustrated by Zena Flax

CHELSEA JUNIORS
A division of Chelsea House Publishers
New York · Philadelphia

Contents

First Printing

1 3 5 7 9 8 6 4 2

ISBN 0-7910-1515-7

Preface

Nature is everywhere, even in towns. Interesting plants thrive on neglected walls. Frogs survive in garden ponds. Chaffinches compete with sparrows for picnic crumbs in parks. Foxes, attracted from the countryside by easy pickings of scrap food out of our bulging garbage tins, dig underground shelters in overgrown gardens and watch their cubs at play on well-kept lawns. Many of the activities in this book can be done in town or country. With few exceptions, they are about wonders to be seen in commonplace things – if only you take time and patience to look and see. They will make you aware of how nature interconnects with human life. Perhaps they will make you think about how you too are a part of nature – a human animal.

Science is about making observations, asking questions and seeking answers through making fair tests (experimenting), but observation is the key to good scientific knowledge and understanding. Nature study is filled with fascinating opportunities for making your own discoveries through observation. Nature is especially interesting because plants and animals are alive. But this also means that you need to take care not to harm living things without a good reason. It is not a good reason to kill a spider just because you hate "creepy crawlies", but it might be a good reason to spray crops to kill insects, because people who are starving need the crops for food.

Most of the activities in this book are about learning science through the practice of observation. The materials you need should be easy to find at home. Broad-bean, mustard and cress seeds can be purchased from a garden supply shop. Reference books borrowed from a library will help you to name the plants and animals you see. Studying nature is fairly safe, unless you try to eat strange plants, including berries and fungi. Wash your hands after handling unfamiliar plants and always after handling animals. Cuckoo-pints and foxgloves, mentioned in this book, are poisonous. Be careful when you explore near deep water or climb trees – and don't risk climbing cliffs. Wild animals bite and injuries can be infected by unpleasant germs. Beware of poisonous snakes. (Take care when you are turning over stones in open country.) There is no reason why you should actually kill a poisonous snake – unless careless people, particularly other children, are really in danger.

Living worlds in dead trees

An old log of dead wood is a living community of plants and animals. Look on rotting tree-trunks and fallen branches, to find lichens and fungi. Break off a piece of crumbling bark. It has lots of holes where the rot-softened wood is eaten away by worm-like beetle larvae.

The caps of fungi, shaped like umbrellas and shelf-brackets, colored grey, white, orange or fawn, are the spore-making, reproductive parts of these "plants without green chlorophyll". Unlike green plants, fungi cannot make food from air, water and soil nutrients, and so they feed on the food accumulated in the remains of dead things.

Just underneath the bark you may find tangled mats of delicate, whitish hyphae. These are the feeding parts of fungi, that grew from spores that got in through holes in the bark bored by insects. Hyphae penetrate and digest the wood, changing it into a pulpy substance. Small creatures bore into the soft wood, some of which they eat. The rest of the wood gets turned into small pieces that help to make rich soil from which new plants grow.

Several kinds of fungus are luminous. If you spend some time at night, getting your eyes used to pitch darkness, you may be able to see the ghostly luminescence coming from some dead wood.

Lichens are two-in-one plants . . . . Every kind is really a living combination of a fungus and a simple type of green plant called an alga. The fungus absorbs water and nutrient, and the alga makes food from these substances and air – to be shared with the fungus. Lichens are flaky-textured and withered-looking, colored grey, brown and black. You have seen the brilliant orange lichens growing on stonework. Plenty of lichen growth is a sign that the air is free from serious pollution.

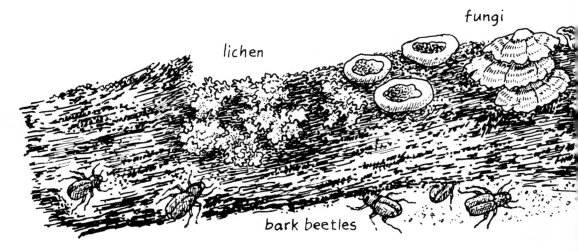

fungi

lichen

bark beetles

Females of various sorts of bark beetles lay their
eggs in tunnels that they chew away, just underneath
the bark. Look for these bark beetle galleries. They
have side branches that get progressively wider.
Can you guess why? You will be certain to find
galleries made by elm-bark beetles. These beetles
carry the spores of the Dutch elm disease fungus that
has killed millions of elm trees.

Legs galore

Do you know the difference between centipedes and
millipedes? Both can be found in rotting trees. They
are worm-like creatures with a lot of legs, but never as
many as a hundred (centi) or thousand (milli). They
are dark-reddish and yellowish-brown animals, with
bodies composed of many segments (divisions),
protected – as are insects – by coverings of shell-like
chitin.

Millipedes are slower than centipedes and have two
pairs of legs per segment – centipedes have one pair.
Millipedes feed on plant material and are a garden
pest. Centipedes are carnivorous, feeding on small
insects and larvae. Both prefer dark, damp places
and are, therefore, secretive. Find some and study
how they move. Look for a mother centipede inside a
rotten log. You may find her curled around her eggs.
She will care for her young for some time, after they
hatch. By the way, some centipedes are luminous . . .
(Any theories?)

elm-bark beetle
galleries
and
elm-bark
beetle

centipede

millipede

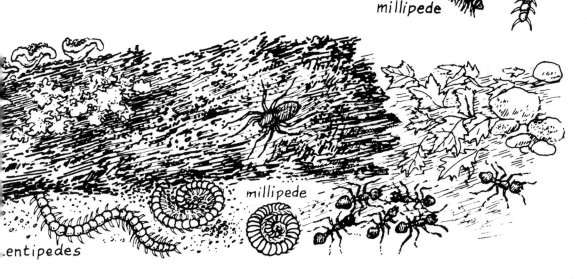

millipede

entipedes

A spider safari

Spiders are different from insects. An insect has three pairs of legs and a segmented body divided into head, thorax (middle part) and abdomen. A spider has a cephalothorax (head and thorax combined), an abdomen and four pairs of legs. Spiders may have as many as eight eyes, although their eyesight is generally poor. All spiders spin silk, called gossamer. It is used to make life-lines, webs and silky egg cocoons – but not all spiders spin webs.

House spider

Many people are scared by the fearsome-looking house spider that gets trapped inside the slippery-sided bathtub while searching for water. Yet inventors have made "spider-tongs" and miniature "rope"-ladders, to rescue spiders from baths. At night-time the house spider prowls about our rooms, moving as quickly as a mouse. Look for its untidy cobwebs that gather dust behind furniture.

Garden spider

Watch a green and cross-marked garden spider spinning its attractive orb web. First it lets out a silk line, to be blown by the breeze, to span a wide gap – and it finishes by making a spiral of silk, beaded with glue-like drops to which the netted insects stick.

Sensitive hairs on the spider's body detect the shaking web lines when a struggling fly, bee or butterfly is caught. Discover how the spider binds its victims in silk, to eat or rather drink them later . . .

The spider's hollow fangs are used to inject poison, which makes the prey helpless – and liquifies the inner parts of the body, to be sucked out later.

You can get an orb web to stick to a piece of cardboard. Gently spray a web with paint from an aerosol tin. Spray the web and one side of the card with hair spray. Quickly press the wet cardboard against the web. The web sticks to the card and can be taken away.

paint

hair spray

card

You can set up a vivarium (living space) for a house or garden spider, inside an old aquarium. Put in a floor of damp soil or leaf-mold. Include a dish of water, a short cardboard tube and a framework of twigs. Keep your pet for two or three days for close observation. It should spin a web. You can put in a live fly or two, but your spider will not starve if you release it soon.

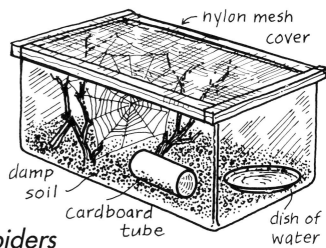

nylon mesh cover

damp soil

Cardboard tube

dish of water

Zebra and wolf spiders

jumping zebra spider

You may find the tiny black-and-white-striped zebra spider basking on a sunny windowsill. It is a good jumper and pounces on its small prey like a cat. Look in the garden for another good jumper, the roving wolf spider. Search for a female, rolling a silken cocoon that holds her eggs. When the spiderlings hatch she will let them ride on her back.

On a late summer day the spiderlings will spin long threads, which catch the wind, to carry the little spiders away – "ballooning" – to colonize distant places.

wolf spider

wolf spider with eggs

spiderling ready for ballooning

Jungle war in the rose-bush

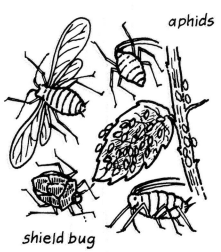

aphids

shield bug

The enemy

Early summer is the time when hordes of plant-lice, called aphids, invade our gardens. They belong to a group of insects which includes frog-hoppers, the aptly-named plant-sucking shield bugs and water-boatmen. All the insects in this group have mouth-parts made in various forms of long beaks, and these are used for piercing the skins of plants and animals, to suck vital juices. Aphids are commonly known as blackflies, that infest broad beans, and greenflies, that smother the roses – and damage other plants, too.

Look for the female, winged forms of these insects. You may discover some clinging to washing hung out to dry. When an aphid settles on a stem, it starts to give birth to many wingless daughters – each of which starts to suck plant juice. As the babies feed and grow, they get sticky with sugary "honey-dew" that they excrete with the waste from their bodies. Look closely at cars parked in hot weather beneath lime and sycamore trees. You may see drops of honey-dew that have rained down from plant-lice feeding on the leaf sap overhead. Observe garden ants, usually in pairs, fussing round flocks of sap-sucking greenflies. The ants enjoy licking the tasty honey-dew. They even take aphids into their underground nests, to protect them during the winter.

Find a single fat greenfly that is walking about freely. Put it on a well-washed rose stem – and keep it inside a glass tube. Count how many babies appear after one, then after two days. Watch a greenfly giving birth. During the summer, daughter greenflies can all give birth to babies – without the attentions of a male insect.

A gardener's allies

Aphids make juicy food for many other animals, such as blue tits that have large summer families to feed. Some of the most interesting predators, that prey on aphids, are other insects.

The seven-spot ladybug is particularly voracious. Gently catch one and let it crawl up your finger. Watch its colorful forewings (actually serving as wing covers) rise and stick out sideways, while its main wings unfurl, before the red beetle flies away.

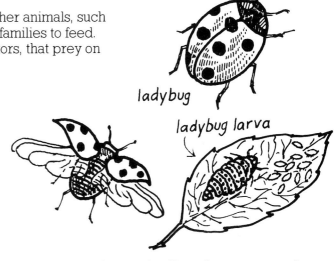

ladybug

ladybug larva

Observe these insects feeding where masses of aphids are busy. Both the adult ladybug and its dark-green-bodied, yellow-spotted larvae munch up many aphids every day. Look for them on rose bushes. The seven-spot ladybug is strong enough to support a force of 800 times its own weight – the equivalent of a small child being safely run over by a double-decker bus. You may find ladybugs hibernating in a hedge in winter.

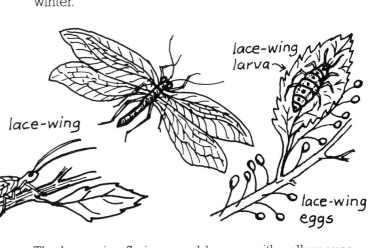

lace-wing larva

lace-wing

lace-wing eggs

The lace-wing fly is emerald green with yellow eyes and beautifully veined, transparent wings. You may have seen one sheltering indoors in the autumn. It would be wonderful if you could see one laying eggs – each one on a little stalk – in clusters, on a rose stem. Lace-wing larvae have sharp jaws to chew up lots of aphids.

Life in a vermarium

Charles Darwin, the main proposer of the theory of evolution, thought that earthworms were very important. They help to drain and aerate the ground, and they enrich the soil by pulling down and digesting fresh and rotting leaves. In this way they restore the chemical richness of the earth for new plants. Darwin reckoned that every worm lifts and turns about one pound of earth a year – so your garden is dug over, whether you like it or not.

Study earthworms at work in a vermarium (an underground living space for worms). You need a large sweet-jar, some rich, loamy soil and some washed sand. Fill the jar with alternate layers of sand and soil, making sure that the vermarium is moist – but never waterlogged. (Have you noticed how heavy rain drives worms from their holes, even out into the road?) Put about six worms inside your jar.

Feed your pets with a few dead leaves, plant remains or grass cuttings. They will haul these into their burrows, by gripping them with their mouths – at their pointed ends. Find out what sorts of vegetable foods your earthworms prefer. They are supposed to be fond of beech leaves.

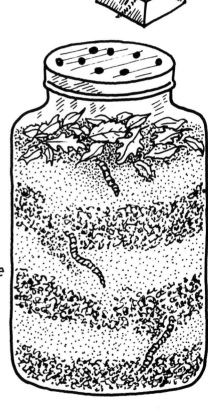

Keep the jar in a cool place and cover it with a black paper tube.

worm casts

The worms both burrow and literally eat their way through the soil. It contains bits of plant remains that they digest. While the worms tunnel about, the soil gets mixed up – as you will see when the soil and sand layers in the jar are well disturbed. Look for worm-casts made up of coils of molded soil, excreted above ground.

The bisexual (two-sexed) earthworm

Earthworms are hermaphrodites – every worm plays the part of both male and female. In wet weather you may have seen two worms stuck together by the wide swollen rings on their many-segmented bodies. They were mating.

Each worm fertilizes the eggs of the other. After the earthworms separate, the bands slide forward along their bodies, to become little lemon-shaped cocoons that contain a few eggs.

Sounds and movements

Stand your vermarium on top of a piano and play some bass notes. Earthworms are sensitive to vibrations, such as those caused in the ground by falling rain. Your pets may appear from their holes.

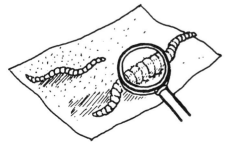

On the underside of most segments a worm has stiff hairs called setae. When it wants to move in a tunnel, the worm reaches forward, anchors itself by its fore-end setae – then pulls itself along. You can observe how a worm moves over very rough paper. Listen for the faint scratching sound it makes.

Keep a colony of wood-lice

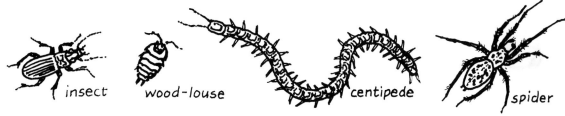

insect   wood-louse   centipede   spider

Wood-lice, spiders, centipedes and insects are separate groups of cold-blooded animals without backbones. They are divisions of one of the main groups of animals, called Arthropoda – sharing the common characteristic of having jointed legs. (A person with *arthritis* has an inflammation of the joints, and a stand upon three legs is called a tri*pod*.) Wood-lice, like beetles, fungi and countless billions of germ-like microbes, play their part in breaking down dead matter. In this way the world is not cluttered with dead bodies – and chemicals needed for new growth are given back to nature.

Wood-lice are common under loose bark on decaying trees, beneath stones and down amongst leaf litter and the matted parts of plants. Amazingly, they are related to water-dwelling crabs and lobsters – they even breathe with gills (not lungs) which they must keep damp, to absorb oxygen from the air. That is why you will nearly always find wood-lice in damp places.

Put ten wood-lice into a closed tin, the bottom of which is half covered with damp blotting paper, the other half with dry paper – and see what happens.

lid

dry paper

tin

damp blotting paper

Although many sorts of wood-lice are found in the woods, you will probably recognize two main types – the flat wood-louse and the pill-louse. Touch a pill-louse and watch it curl into a ball, like a hedgehog. Perhaps this habit also helps to conserve its moisture. At one time pill-lice were taken as pills, to "cure" diseases.

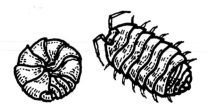

The outer skin of a wood-louse does not grow. A soft and stretchy new skin grows underneath. Then the outer skin is shed or moulted. Look for a wood-louse that is half pale-colored. It is moulting. The skin splits across the middle. First the wood-louse crawls out of the rear part, then, after a few days' rest, it backs out of the front part. Meanwhile, the new skin gets harder and darkens to brown or grey. Nothing is wasted though, for the wood-louse eats its own shed skin.

moulting wood-louse

Handle delicate wood-lice – and other small animals – with the aid of a water-color brush and a plastic spoon.

Put a wood-louse on its back and watch, to see how it turns the right way over. Watch how the wood-louse moves its antennae (feelers). Observe its scaly back. Count its legs. How does it walk? Study its head, tail and softer underparts, using a magnifying-glass. Underneath, you may see a brood-pouch (a swelling between the legs), where a mother wood-louse stores her eggs, and keeps the young animals for some days after they hatch.

Keep a colony for observation in a shallow dish, lined with damp compost and rotting leaves. They appreciate a piece of bark to hide under. Being nocturnal (belonging to the night) they will not be very active during the day. Try to observe a wood-louse eating, or digging itself into the ground.

Wood-lice prefer dark to light places – and they like to rest with their sides touching upright surfaces. Do some experiments to see if these assertions are true.

Attracting garden birds

When you make a special effort to identify the types of birds that inhabit your neighborhood, you will begin to recognize individual birds as old friends, and you will find yourself noticing interesting details about their behavior. You can start by taking a little trouble to attract birds to your garden – even if you live in a town and the garden is only a small yard.

Build a bird-feeder by nailing a large tray on top of a tall and unpainted wooden post that is standing up firmly in the ground – and out of reach of the local cats. Birds appreciate drinking facilities, and a place to bathe, so use (or make) a tray that is big and strong enough to support a shallow dish of water, which you must not allow to get too dirty.

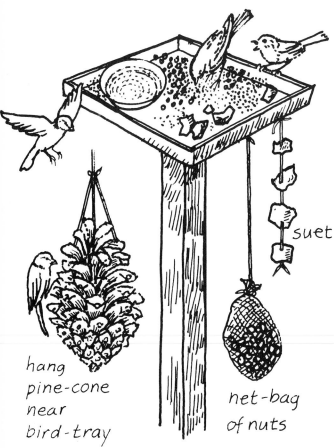

hang
pine-cone
near
bird-tray

net-bag
of nuts

suet

Start to feed the birds in early autumn, and keep putting out fresh food throughout the winter. Provide more variety than bread-crumbs. Avoid salty things. Various species of birds will eat boiled potato, melon and sunflower seeds, crushed dog-biscuit, chopped apple and oatmeal.

Smear a paste of bird-seed and peanut butter amongst the bracts of a pine-cone suspended from a string. Other things to hang up are crusts of bread and the hard animal fat – from a butcher's – known as suet. You can also buy a net-bag of nuts to hang under the tray.

Do not put your feeding station where birds will be continually disturbed by people. You might be able to convert a nearby window into a viewing "blind," by fixing up a sheet of cardboard with a slot to look through.

Questions and observations

Get to know the names of the birds that visit your bird-feeder. Use a good book with color pictures. Visitors may include the robin, house sparrow, chaffinch, greenfinch, starling, blackbird and dunnock or "hedge sparrow". Other visitors will depend on where you live and the time of the year. Activity will be brisk during severe weather – you can consider designing a bird-feeder with a roof.

tape cardboard over window – cut small viewing hole in cardboard

Notice how the different species approach your feeding station. Do they fly up from the ground, from shrubbery nearby, or do they fly directly down? Do they come alone, or in groups? Which types of birds are "bullies"? How well do the birds get on with each other? Does a bird have a special way of eating its food? Is there a connection between birds' beaks and the foods they choose?

You will admire the agility of blue tits, clinging upside-down from the suet. Do birds "line up" for turns on the net-bag of nuts? Notice how birds move on the ground. Do they run or hop? The flights of a collared dove or an exultant pigeon can be sheer joy to watch. These birds must surely take pleasure in flight for its own sake.

Remarkable observations on birds

A naturalist noticed a large "green snake", flecked with red, moving on a sandy embankment. It proved to be a crooked line of 23 green woodpeckers feeding on ants from numerous ants' nests.

The green woodpecker has a sticky tongue, longer than its head, which it can poke into holes in the ground, in search of ants. The insects stick to its tongue as if it were flypaper. You are unlikely to see anything like the woodpecker "snake", but you might see a nervous woodpecker hunting for ants infesting your lawn. It has a ringing, laughing cry. It is supposed to be particularly noisy before bad weather.

You may notice some remarkable stories in newspapers and magazines. For several days, scientists in England who were watching Russian television beamed down from a satellite, noticed that the TV screen went fuzzy every day at 10 minutes past 4. On investigation, they found that a great tit was using a hole in the base of their dish-shaped aerial as its night-time roosting place.

Crows are known for their antics. In one incident, the big black birds "dive-bombed" children eating their mid-morning snacks – they perched on the children's shoulders and even tapped on the classroom windows.

One day a naturalist watched a wren "playing" with a vole. The vole, a small, short-tailed rodent, was making a nest. Every time the vole crossed a little open space, the wren perched on its back and rode along until it was knocked off by the entrance to the vole's burrow.

Sometimes scientists set problems for birds to solve. Birds in the tit family are good at this. The picture shows one of these tests. The bird must get the food (a nut or a lump of suet) out of the transparent tube, by pulling the string. Try this on birds that visit your garden to feed.

Look out for these –
and make your own discoveries

A well-known deformity in starlings is an abnormally long, curving beak – like a curlew's. This sometimes happens when the bottom part of the beak gets damaged and the top part just keeps on growing.

A blue tit was once observed pecking through milk-bottle caps and taking the cream off the top of the milk. Blue tits are quick learners, and so the trick soon spread. Look out for this.

By day, a tawny owl rests in a wood, perched close to a tree-trunk. If discovered by smaller birds – who have good reasons to dislike owls – the owl is mobbed. Watch for an owl at the center of a commotion.

A magpie resents other species of birds in its territory. You may see, or hear, a magpie being aggressive to a jay, a woodpecker, or even an owl. But the gentle-looking collared dove can chase away a bullying magpie.

There may be a quiet spot in your garden where birds like to sunbathe in hot weather. The wing feathers are spread out in a relaxed way, and the bird's beak is half-opened. It pants like a dog to lose heat.

These interesting observations are not rare, so you have a good chance of seeing them. If you do see anything unusual, write to your local newspaper. It's fun to see your own name in print.

Your own nature trail

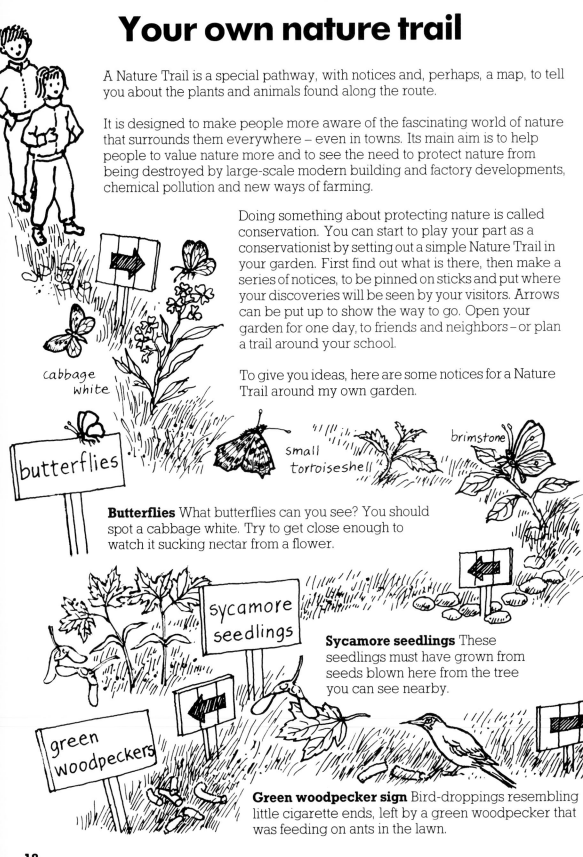

A Nature Trail is a special pathway, with notices and, perhaps, a map, to tell you about the plants and animals found along the route.

It is designed to make people more aware of the fascinating world of nature that surrounds them everywhere – even in towns. Its main aim is to help people to value nature more and to see the need to protect nature from being destroyed by large-scale modern building and factory developments, chemical pollution and new ways of farming.

Doing something about protecting nature is called conservation. You can start to play your part as a conservationist by setting out a simple Nature Trail in your garden. First find out what is there, then make a series of notices, to be pinned on sticks and put where your discoveries will be seen by your visitors. Arrows can be put up to show the way to go. Open your garden for one day, to friends and neighbors – or plan a trail around your school.

To give you ideas, here are some notices for a Nature Trail around my own garden.

cabbage white

butterflies

small tortoiseshell

brimstone

Butterflies What butterflies can you see? You should spot a cabbage white. Try to get close enough to watch it sucking nectar from a flower.

sycamore seedlings

Sycamore seedlings These seedlings must have grown from seeds blown here from the tree you can see nearby.

green woodpeckers

Green woodpecker sign Bird-droppings resembling little cigarette ends, left by a green woodpecker that was feeding on ants in the lawn.

Galls on sycamore leaves
The ugly spots and pimples on the leaves grew around eggs laid inside the leaves by insects. The larvae will feed on the tree.

galls

thrush's anvil

Thrush's anvil Notice the broken snail-shells around this stone. They were smashed by a song-thrush getting out the snail meat.

wolf spiders

Wolf spiders Look around here to find a female wolf spider carrying a silk ball she spun herself, to contain her eggs.

wolf spider with eggs

cuckoo-spit

frog-hopper

Cuckoo-spit This bubbly froth is made by the nymph (immature form) of a plant bug called a frog-hopper. Protected by the froth, the nymph is feeding by sucking juices from the stem.

weeds

Weeds Weeds are just flowers in the wrong place. Look around for groundsel, chickweed, dandelions, shepherd's purse and daisies.

hover-flies

Hover-flies Although these black and yellow striped insects look like wasps, they are harmless. Some kinds have larvae that eat greenflies. (What are these adult flies feeding on?) Do take time to admire their flying skills.

Weeds are flowers too

Do you know the names of the wild flowers that grow in your garden? Yes, you recognize the dandelion, daisy, buttercup, thistle, and clover.

Make up your mind to learn the names of some other common garden weeds – many of which have forgotten uses as vegetables and medicines.

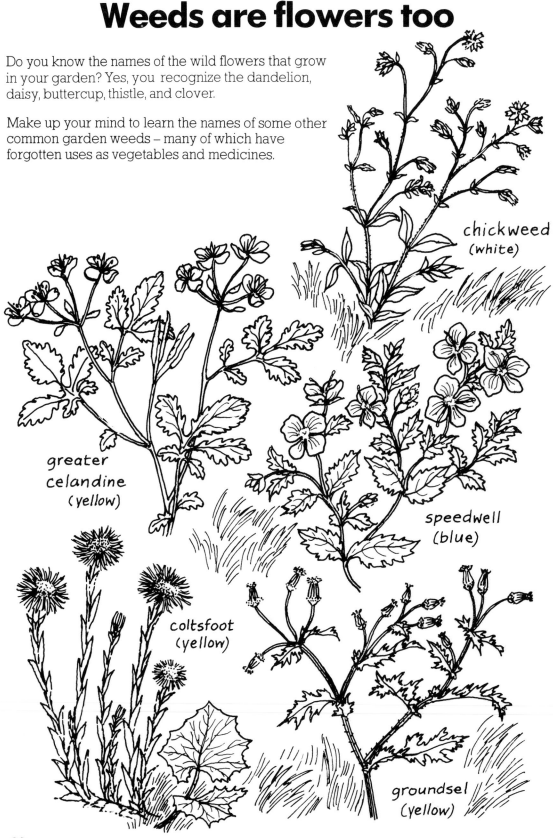

chickweed
(white)

greater
celandine
(yellow)

speedwell
(blue)

coltsfoot
(yellow)

groundsel
(yellow)

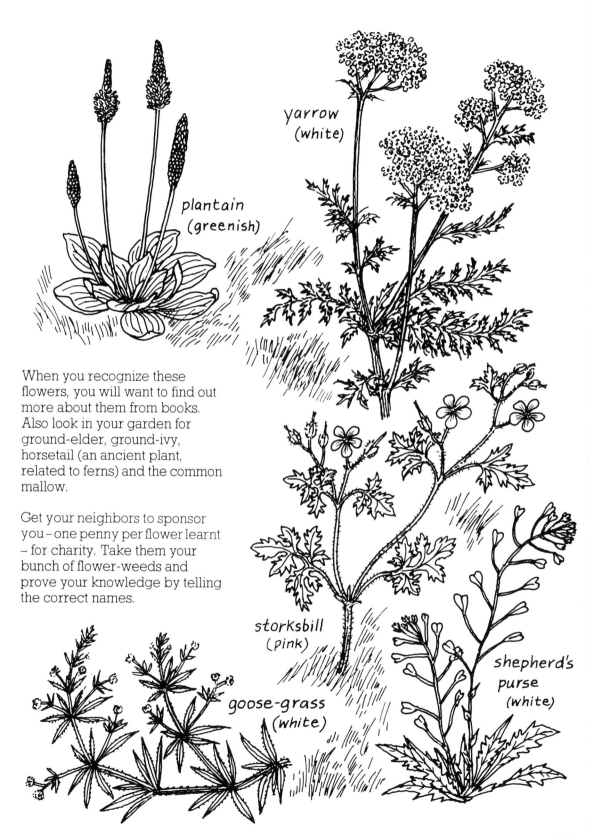

plantain
(greenish)

yarrow
(white)

When you recognize these
flowers, you will want to find out
more about them from books.
Also look in your garden for
ground-elder, ground-ivy,
horsetail (an ancient plant,
related to ferns) and the common
mallow.

Get your neighbors to sponsor
you – one penny per flower learnt
– for charity. Take them your
bunch of flower-weeds and
prove your knowledge by telling
the correct names.

storksbill
(pink)

goose-grass
(white)

shepherd's
purse
(white)

Meet the dandelion

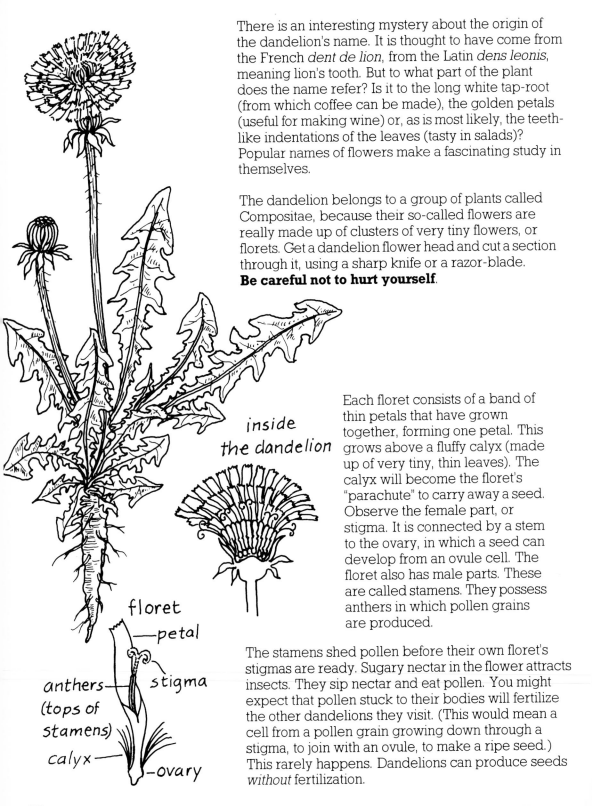

There is an interesting mystery about the origin of the dandelion's name. It is thought to have come from the French *dent de lion*, from the Latin *dens leonis*, meaning lion's tooth. But to what part of the plant does the name refer? Is it to the long white tap-root (from which coffee can be made), the golden petals (useful for making wine) or, as is most likely, the teeth-like indentations of the leaves (tasty in salads)? Popular names of flowers make a fascinating study in themselves.

The dandelion belongs to a group of plants called Compositae, because their so-called flowers are really made up of clusters of very tiny flowers, or florets. Get a dandelion flower head and cut a section through it, using a sharp knife or a razor-blade. **Be careful not to hurt yourself**.

inside the dandelion

floret

—petal

anthers—
(tops of
stamens)

stigma

calyx—

—ovary

Each floret consists of a band of thin petals that have grown together, forming one petal. This grows above a fluffy calyx (made up of very tiny, thin leaves). The calyx will become the floret's "parachute" to carry away a seed. Observe the female part, or stigma. It is connected by a stem to the ovary, in which a seed can develop from an ovule cell. The floret also has male parts. These are called stamens. They possess anthers in which pollen grains are produced.

The stamens shed pollen before their own floret's stigmas are ready. Sugary nectar in the flower attracts insects. They sip nectar and eat pollen. You might expect that pollen stuck to their bodies will fertilize the other dandelions they visit. (This would mean a cell from a pollen grain growing down through a stigma, to join with an ovule, to make a ripe seed.) This rarely happens. Dandelions can produce seeds *without* fertilization.

How the dandelion is such a good survivor

The dandelion is a very persistent weed. It blooms from spring to well into autumn. Its numerous seeds can travel for miles on the wind, but a new plant can also grow quickly from any healthy part of its root that is left in the ground, after the top of the plant has been cut off by a lawn-mower. Break off the above-ground part of a dandelion plant, mark the spot, and see how long it takes to produce flowers again. Flowers will bud very close to the ground.

Spread out 25 freshly-plucked seeds (from a "dandelion clock") on damp blotting-paper, inside a transparent plastic lunch-box. Keep the lid on and store in a warm place, out of direct sunlight. Watch every day, to see how the seeds germinate (start to grow). How many seeds are viable? That is, how many actually grow into seedlings? Compare the viability of seeds from different dandelion plants.

Observe the fine root-hairs that absorb moisture. Roots are protected on their tips by tough root-caps. The roots grow with a spiraling motion – which helps them to bore through the ground and to avoid stones.

dandelion 'parachute'

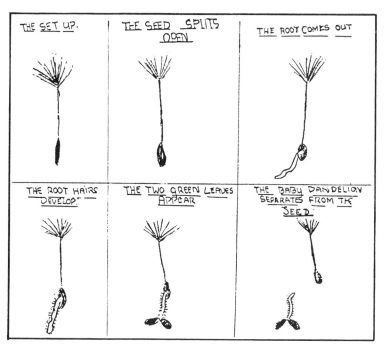

THE SET UP.

THE SEED SPLITS OPEN

THE ROOT COMES OUT

THE ROOT HAIRS DEVELOP.

THE TWO GREEN LEAVES APPEAR

THE BABY DANDELION SEPARATES FROM THE SEED.

Drawings by a group of children who did the experiment described.

Make a salad from well-washed, fresh, young leaves, mixed with vegetables and seasoning.

How plants get their water

Soak a ripe cherry in water. It swells and splits. Why? The cherry skin is perforated with very tiny holes. They are smaller than the big "cherry molecules" inside, but not too small to stop water molecules from passing to and fro. More water goes into the cherry than gets out – because outward passage is blocked by the bigger molecules. So, inside the fruit, pressure builds up until the cherry bursts.

When more water goes in than comes out through a porous membrane (skin) that shuts in large molecules, the process is called osmosis.

Osmosis helps to explain how water and small molecules of minerals, dissolved from the soil, can get in through the membranes which surround root-hair cells of plants. Osmosis also helps you to understand how molecules of digested (broken-down) food can get through membranes lining your intestine, into your bloodstream.

But what makes molecules move? The answer is their temperature. They will generally be slightly warm. Heat makes all molecules, large and small, jiggle to and fro in a kind of vibration. Small molecules can jiggle, or diffuse their way through the porous membrane, but big molecules cannot – they jiggle against the edges of the holes and act like valves, making the passage *mainly* one way.

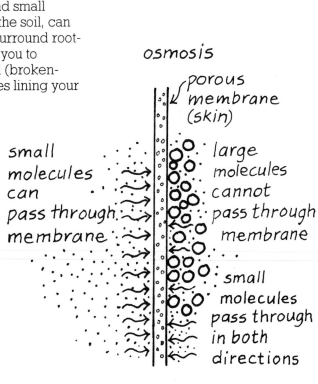

osmosis

porous membrane (skin)

small molecules can pass through membrane

large molecules cannot pass through membrane

small molecules pass through in both directions

24

Demonstrations of osmosis

Slice the top and bottom off a potato. Shave off about a half-inch width of the skin around the lower edge. Hollow out a thimble-size well at the top and stand the potato in a saucer of water. Put a little thick sugar and water solution inside the well – and wait.

large molecules inside potato

thick sugar and water solution (large sugar molecules)

clear water (small water molecules)

Large molecules of substances, such as starch, inside the cells at the bottom of the potato restrict the amount of water that can pass out through the cell wall membranes, and so more water goes into the cells, increasing the pressure inside them – and weakening the concentration of large molecules. Inside the potato, more water can go from cells containing weak concentrations of large molecules into cells in which concentrations are greater – therefore, water penetrates and rises up towards the cells that line the well. But there the concentration of large sugar molecules in water is so great that water can pass out through the cell membranes into the sugar solution. This increases the amount of water in the well and might cause it to overflow.

Cut two equal-sized, raw french fries. Put one in water and the other in strong salt solution. Explain why one swells and gets stiff, while the other shrinks and gets flabby.

french fry

water

french fry

strong salt solution

Make long cuts up from the bottom of a dandelion stem. Leave it in water. The ends curl like springs. Can you explain this?

Another way to describe osmosis is to say that, when a weak and a strong solution are separated by a membrane that will let only smaller molecules pass through (a semi-permeable membrane), water and dissolved minerals will pass into the stronger solution, making it weaker. This sets up "osmotic pressure".

Tricks with plants

Green plants need water to make food, to transport food and chemicals in solution to their various parts, and to keep them standing erect, with leaves that do not droop. Water must be able to get through a plant. Water that enters root-hairs travels in towards the stem by osmotic action. It then gets into very thin tubes that rise all the way up to the leaves, where there are openings through which water can evaporate.

Evaporating water causes suction in the tubes. Forces between the water molecules and the linings of the tubes help the water to climb in continuous streams. These forces, aided by suction and by osmotic pressure from below, are mainly responsible for keeping the flow going.

strong
food
coloring
in water

coloring
has dyed
the celery

To get a rough idea of what must be going on in a stem, stand a fresh stick of celery in a jar containing a strong solution of food coloring. After a day or two, cut across the stem. You will see a pattern of cells stained by the dye, showing that water has travelled upwards.

Patriotic carnations

The picture shows you how to create a red, white and blue carnation, by splitting the stem of a white flower, before standing each part in food coloring of water. Before doing these experiments cut the bottoms of the stems *underwater.* Do not let bubbles of air get in.

split stem

blue dye

red dye

clear water

26

Towards a "Great Bean Race"

Seeds need oxygen from air, warmth and moisture – and they may need darkness – if they are to germinate, or commence to grow. At first, they rely on food that was stored inside them by the parent plant, but after the first green leaves appear, they can manufacture their own food from carbon dioxide gas in the air, water, and minerals dissolved from their surroundings.

Stuff two or three water-soaked broad-bean seeds between the glass wall of a jar and wads of damp paper. Eventually, shoots appear and grow upwards – away from the pull of gravity. And roots grow downwards – towards where gravity seems to act. Then turn the jar upside-down for a day or two – and see how well the beans can sense gravitational change.

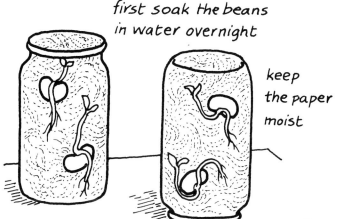

first soak the beans in water overnight

keep the paper moist

Plant a bean in a pot of compost. When its shoot appears, put the pot inside a sub-divided cardboard box, where holes have been cut in the divisions to make a maze. Keep the plant watered, but let it grow in darkness. The exit should face a window. How long does the bean take to reach the light? Make two mazes and hold a "Great Bean Race".

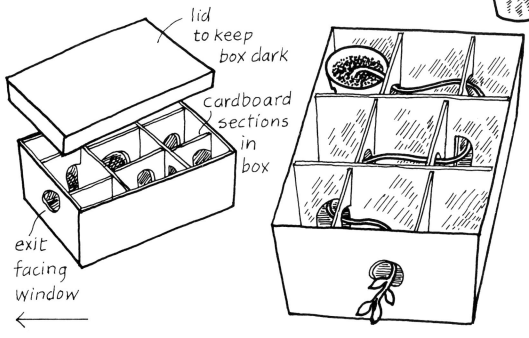

lid to keep box dark

cardboard sections in box

exit facing window

Wonders of pollination

Cross-pollination is the way that flowers can share their slightly different characteristics with their offspring. The cuckoo-pint has an amazing way of being cross-pollinated. It has separate, wart-like male and female flowers, shut inside a tube formed from the base of a greenish trumpet. In the middle of the trumpet is a purplish spike, smelling of rotten meat – a lure to attract small insects.

Long, drooping bristles, just inside the slippery top of the tube, allow insects to enter – but the insects are trapped and fall past a lesser barrier of bristles, to a bottom chamber that contains the female flowers. Any cuckoo-pint pollen grains on the insects' bodies are accidentally rubbed on to the stigmas of the flowers. Then, on each pollinated stigma, a male cell from a pollen grain can grow through the stigma, to fertilize a female ovule cell inside the flower's ovary. The ovule becomes a seed and the ovary changes into a fruity berry. After pollination the stigmas exude sugary nectar. This is consumed by the insects.

When the female flowers have stopped being receptive to pollen, the plant's own male flowers start to shower pollen over the imprisoned insects. All this time the air inside the plant is nearly 18°F warmer than the outside air. Warmth is probably needed to evaporate "smell molecules" from the purple spike – to spread the smell. Eventually, the plant cools, the smell fades and the bristles wither. After a day or so the insects can escape to pollinate another plant.

In the spring, find and cut open a cuckoo-pint. Do you find little flies and beetles inside? You can also investigate temperatures inside cuckoo-pints. The beautiful scarlet berries that are ripe by autumn are poisonous. As children, we used to call them snakes' food.

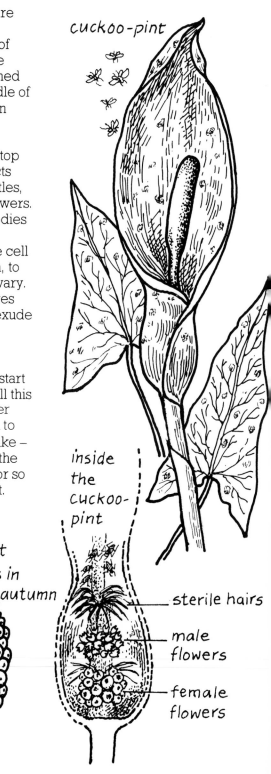

cuckoo-pint

inside the cuckoo-pint

scarlet berries in autumn

sterile hairs

male flowers

female flowers

Foxgloves and bumble-bees

Look for purple foxgloves in the late summer. Flower buds open in the order from bottom to top, as you can check. This coincides with the bumble-bee's habit of going to the bottom flowers first, then working its way up. Blooming in two stages, starting from the bottom of a plant, also helps its flowers to be cross-pollinated. Their stamens do not droop and release pollen, until after their stigmas have received pollen from other foxglove plants, brought by bees. So a bee bringing pollen from flowers at the top of a plant is likely to pollinate flowers on another plant.

The tube-shaped flowers develop in two stages. Female stigmas are ready first. They droop, to be in a position to touch the back of a visiting bee that may have foxglove pollen sticking to it. Later the stigmas are raised. Then the pollen-bearing stamens are ready. They also droop, to be in the way of any bumble-bee pushing deep into the flower to reach the nectary.

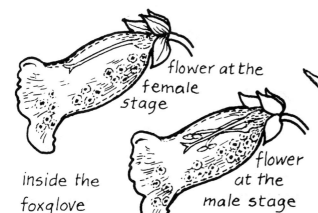

flower at the female stage

inside the foxglove

flower at the male stage

Look for bumble-bee workers. They are female bees, but unable to breed. Watch them gathering foxglove pollen and nectar. They will take them back to their bee colony, to feed the queen bee and their larvae. Look for the "pollen baskets" on a bee's back legs. Foxgloves are shaped to admit bumble-bees. Honey-bees cannot reach the nectary. Cut open some flowers. What do you think the pattern of spots is for? Are the flowers at the female or male stage? Other names for foxgloves are "fairies' thimbles" and "deadmen's bells". Foxglove plants are poisonous, but doctors know how to use their leaves for treating heart disease.

foxglove

pollen baskets

Indoor farms and gardens

Start a mustard and cress farm. Put clean, damp flannel or paper towels on a tray – and aim to keep it damp (not soaking wet) by regular watering, or spraying. "Plant" the cress three days before the mustard crop. Simply sprinkle the seeds thickly on the moist surface. After about two weeks, both crops should be ready for harvesting.

Let the seeds germinate in a warm cupboard, but put them in a well-lit place as soon as the leaves appear. Do not let them shrivel in direct sunlight. There is green chlorophyll in the leaves which enables the plants to make food for their growth, using carbon dioxide from the air, and water. This process is called photosynthesis (it means "building with light"). Light is the energy needed.

Eat your produce in thin bread-and-butter sandwiches.

Grow a handful of bean shoots in a clean jar. Put the beans inside and cover the jar with a double thickness of muslin, held with a rubber band. Pour warm water through the muslin, to half fill the jar. Rinse gently and tip out the water. Put the jar in a dark, but warm place – and water the seeds by rinsing and draining every morning and evening. After five days or so you can eat your bean shoots raw in a salad. You get them fried with food you buy from your Chinese Take-Away.

Spudnik

Make a living potato monster, using twigs and a "spud" or two. Plant mustard seeds in little holes drilled in the Spudnik's back. There is no need to water him.

Jungle in a jar

Get a big pickles jar or carboy and take time to wash the inside thoroughly. Use a funnel and a cardboard tube to pour in about 1.5 in of washed gravel as drainage, then 1.5 in of broken-up charcoal sticks (from an art shop) as a filter, followed by 3 in depth of potting mixture. While you are buying your sterile (germ-free) soil from a garden center, get the sales assistant to suggest a variety of small plants that will be suitable for an indoor bottle garden.

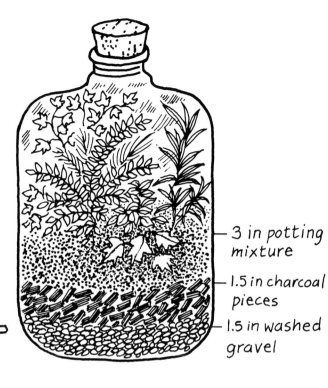

— 3 in potting mixture

— 1.5 in charcoal pieces

— 1.5 in washed gravel

To plant, dig a hole with an old spoon tied to a stick, push down the plant and its clod of soil with an old dinner fork on a stick, then tamp the ground with a stick-handled cotton reel. **Don't get earth on the glass wall**. Use a spray to water the garden – to avoid splashing soil on the glass. Stopper the jar and keep it in a warm, well-lit place, but not in direct sunlight. Water evaporates from the leaves, condenses on the glass, runs down and is recycled through the ground.

You have an enclosed living environment – like a spaceship inside which vital materials are recycled. If there is condensation on more than a third of the glass, open the top, to let some water evaporate.

Water gardens

carrot

beetroot

parsnip

Cut off the tops of vegetables, such as carrots and beetroots. Where the leaves have been removed are little buds. Rest the vegetable tops in water inside dinner plates. Don't use pre-packaged vegetables and do not swamp them with water. Surround them with washed pebbles or colored marbles, keep them in a warm, light place – and watch your gardens grow.

"Animals in slow motion"

Did you know that pansy plants explode? Their fruits stiffen, then they split suddenly – shooting seeds away from the main plant. Listen, on a summer afternoon, to the seed-shedding explosions of juniper on exposed hillsides. Plants can move in all sorts of ways. They have been called "animals in slow motion" – but that is not a very scientific idea.

You have seen how roots and shoots respond to the stimulus of gravity. Cover some growing cress seedlings with a yoghurt pot that has a hole cut in one side – and wait a few days. Then see how they have grown towards the light. This is called phototropism or heliotropism (moving towards the sun). Put a jar of freshly-picked wild flowers and leaves, facing away from the light, on a window-sill. Wait a while, to observe how the flowers gradually twist around towards the light.

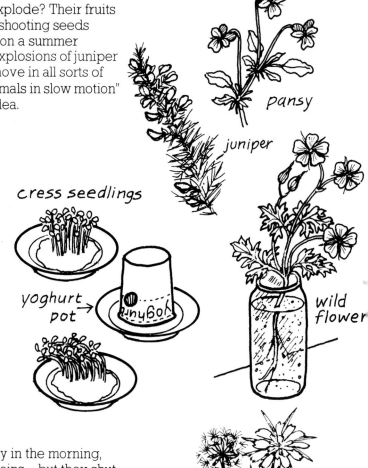

pansy

juniper

cress seedlings

yoghurt pot →

wild flower

Dandelion flowers open very early in the morning, covering a meadow like golden coins – but they shut in the afternoon, apparently disappearing in the green grass. In late summer, the handsome goat's beard, a yellow flower similar to the dandelion, opens at dawn and closes – guess when? Many flowers close during rain or at night, when raindrops or dew can harm their pollen. Bring a closed tulip indoors. It will open within half-an-hour in the warmth. If you keep it in a warm place it just goes on opening and will die before its time. But the petals will close if you put the tulip where it is cool.

goat's beard

tulip's progress

Down in the wood something stirs

wood anemone

tin over wood anemone

In the spring, look for fragile white flowers of the wood anemone. They open in the sunlight, but close and droop when a cloud covers the sun. Put a tin over a wood anemone flower on a sunny day. Wait a little while and see how the flower has moved in the darkness.

wood-sorrel

Wood-sorrel is a very irritable plant. Just stroking its three-lobed leaves makes it fold up. It also responds to nightfall or to too much sunlight.

Plant movements involve bending. Stems, roots, petals and tendrils bend when cells on one side grow slightly faster than cells on the other side. You might be able to buy a sensitive plant (*Mimosa pudica*) at a garden center. Its finely divided leaves close almost instantly when you touch them. Electrical activity stimulates very rapid growth to make this happen.

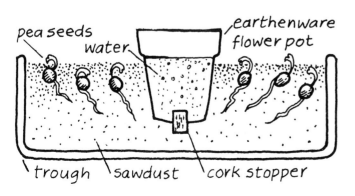

pea seeds

water

earthenware flower pot

trough   sawdust   cork stopper

Hydrotropism

Set up the experiment shown in the picture. Put a blocked-up, porous earthenware flower-pot filled with water in the middle of a trough containing a few pea seeds planted in sawdust. Look for evidence that the roots grow towards the source of the seeping water.

Getting interested in trees

The main living cells of a tree are protected by the rough, tough bark. Just inside the bark is a ring of active cells called the cambium. When cells in the cambium divide into two and multiply, they are pushed either outwards, to strengthen the bark, or inwards, to provide systems of rigid tubes in the sap-wood. The tubes either carry foods, such as sugars manufactured in the leaves, and oxygen down to the lower parts, or they transport water and dissolved chemicals (raw materials for food manufacture) up to the leaves. The liquids flowing in these tubes are called sap.

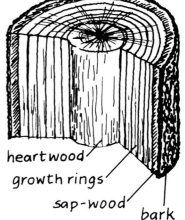

heartwood
growth rings
sap-wood
bark

Each spring the sap-wood thickens – more so if there is plenty of sunshine and rain, less if there is drought or cold. In summer and autumn the growth of sap-wood slows down. Winter is a time of rest. Study clean-cut tree stumps, to see the annual "growth rings" – they are the briefly recorded histories of trees. Count the wider, paler, softer bands of sap-wood, to tell the trees' ages. Ignore the narrow, darker, harder bands of summer and autumn growth. Look for the years of good sun and rain. You may also notice that growth rings are a little wider on the southern, sunnier sides of trees that grew in open spaces.

Apart from their obvious uses as timber and fuel and as providers of fruit and products such as rubber, cork and maple syrup, trees help to make our surroundings more beautiful and interesting. An interest in trees is rewarding. A good way to start is to learn to identify common types of trees growing near your home. (You could borrow a library book about trees, or ask an expert their names.) Make a habit of noticing particular trees whenever you pass them, at whatever time of the year. Observe the ways they change. Notice the sorts of birds that visit them – or grey squirrels. Smell their flowers. Admire the colors of trees that shed their leaves in the autumn. You will never regret taking some trouble to do this.

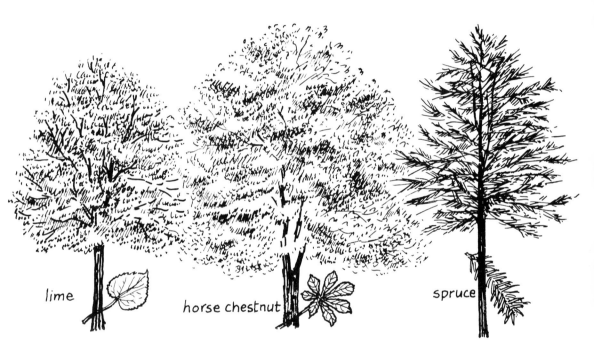

lime

horse chestnut

spruce

Trees as cameras

On a summer afternoon, look under trees for "solar discs". Minute openings amongst dense leaf cover act like the holes in pin-hole cameras. Through each "hole" the sun projects a circular image of itself. Look for these coin-like patches of light on roads, and paths in woods.

Fun with trees

bramble

oak

waxed paper

It will help you to identify trees if you make a collection of leaf prints. Gather the crisp fallen leaves of autumn, or dry out fresh leaves by ironing them gently between sheets of newspaper. (**Be careful with the iron**.) Rub the veiny leaf surfaces with boot polish, then print by pressing their stained sides on paper.

Colored autumn leaves can be preserved for some time by ironing them between two sheets of waxed paper. This seals them inside layers that are beautifully translucent when you display them against the light coming through a window.

Every tree has its characteristic bark pattern. As well as increasing your knowledge of trees, making bark rubbings is a pleasant artistic pastime. Use strong paper and rub quite hard with the round *side* of a waxed crayon – pressing against the bark ridges. Don't spoil your work by poking into the fissures (cracks) and making holes in the paper.

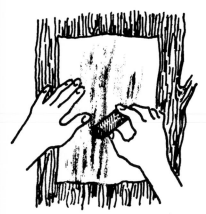

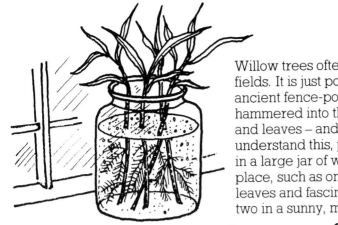

Willow trees often occur in lines along the edges of fields. It is just possible that they sprouted from ancient fence-posts. The still-living green wood, hammered into the ground, produced fresh roots and leaves – and grew into new willow trees. To understand this, put some freshly picked willow twigs in a large jar of water. Kept in an airy, warm, light place, such as on a window-ledge, they will sprout leaves and fascinating underwater roots. Plant one or two in a sunny, moist corner of your garden.

ash keys

cherry stones

hazel nuts

orange pips

conker

acorn

Try to grow little saplings from ash keys, orange pips, cherry stones, hazel nuts, conkers and acorns. Soak all the seeds in water for 24 hours, before planting in pots of moist soil. Hard stones and nuts may be gently cracked first. Don't forget to put small stones or pieces of broken flower-pot into the pots first, to act as drainage. Be patient, keep the soil moist (not waterlogged) and you might get seedlings in a month or two. Rest an acorn or a conker on top of a water-filled bottle, and keep topping up with water – to just wet the seed. You may see an instructive lesson on how these plants germinate.

Birds that nest in trees

Look for big, domed, twiggy magpies' nests, the bare-stick platforms of wood-pigeons (you may see their white eggs showing through the gaps), woodpeckers' holes, and – if you are very fortunate – the huge platform nests of herons. But you must visit a bird sanctuary or nature reserve.

Birds rebuild their old nests and lay their eggs in the Spring. You might catch them stealing sticks from each other. They will certainly be interested in you. Listen to their calls. The young birds will find themselves swinging in the treetops amongst buds that have yet to break out in leaf.

Observing pond-life indoors

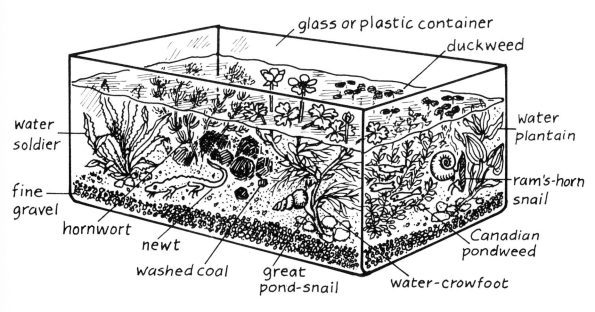

glass or plastic container
duckweed
water plantain
ram's-horn snail
Canadian pondweed
water-crowfoot
great pond-snail
washed coal
newt
hornwort
fine gravel
water soldier

Enjoy a close look at pond-life by setting up an aquarium. Use a glass or a clear plastic container with straight sides. Do not use a goldfish bowl. Wash the container with soapy water and rinse it thoroughly with clean water. Put a layer of well-washed fine gravel on the bottom, but cover this with paper before adding water, to avoid disturbance. Remove the paper afterwards. If tap water is to be used it should be left to stand for several days, to eliminate chlorine gas. You might prefer to use natural pond-water, but you risk having the water contaminated by micro-organisms that might harm or kill your stock.

Pond animals need to breathe, so you must make certain that the water contains enough oxygen. Under ordinary conditions a quantity of oxygen is dissolved from the air, but this does not penetrate far down into the water. If you are not using a mechanical aerator to bubble air through the water, you will need green-leaved pond-plants. They produce oxygen as a by-product of photosynthesis. You can observe bubbles of oxygen coming from pondweeds exposed to sunlight. Gently tie your plants to small stones. Pieces of washed coal make attractive and unusual underwater rocks.

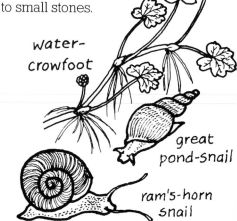

water-crowfoot

great pond-snail

ram's-horn snail

The picture above shows plants to use. If you collect them from a pond, wash them before putting them into your aquarium. Water-snail "scavengers" help to keep the water hygienic, by feeding on decaying matter and microscopic green algae plants that grow on the sides of the aquarium. Don't let the pond-snail eat up all your supply of weed.

Sticklebacks

The male three-spined stickleback has a bluish back and a scarlet belly. It is very aggressive and will attack a red and blue clay model of itself, poked underwater on a thin stick. Put it with two or three duller-colored females. In the spring the male builds a tunnel-nest amongst the weeds. It chases the females inside, fertilizes their eggs – and cares for the hatched young fish, even taking them gently in its mouth and spitting them back into the nest, when they stray. Feed them on blood-worms, chopped meal-worms and water-fleas (daphnia) which you can buy from aquarium shops.

Frogs, toads or newts

Put a *small* quantity of frog or toad spawn into your aquarium. Watch the tadpoles hatch and change, over a period of about three months, into froglets and toadlets. (Keep only three or four animals for prolonged observation – return the other hatched creatures to the pond from which you took the spawn.) Slant sticks in the water, just before the young animals are ready to crawl out of the water. Release them in your garden.

At first, they feed on plants, but later they need to be fed with water-fleas and mosquito wrigglers (underwater larvae).

You may get newts to mate in the spring. The female lays her eggs singly on water-plants. They develop like frogs and toads. Feed newts with mosquito wrigglers and water-fleas.

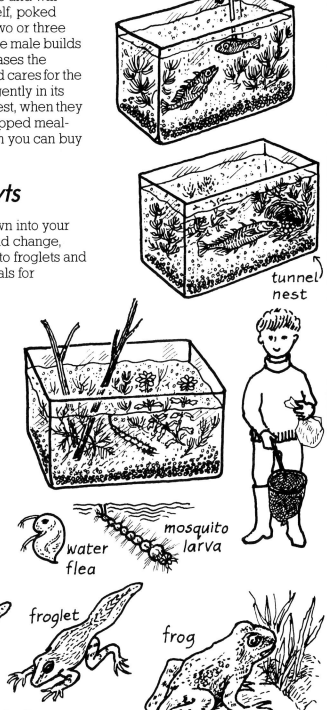

tunnel nest

mosquito larva

water flea

tadpole

froglet

frog

Keep different sorts of animals separately. Put your aquarium in an east- or west-facing window.

Ideas for pond-life studies

Wear old clothes and tall rubber boots when you go on a pond safari and do not go on your own. Take care! Take a strong net, a bucket for animals and plastic bags for water-plants. Back at home, put your finds into pie-dishes, for sorting. Decide which animals you are going to keep for observations, then try to put back into the pond any creatures and plants that you do not need.

Daphnia

These are the so-called "water-fleas" – they seem to hop and jump through the water, but they are really related to lobsters, crayfish and land-dwelling wood-lice. You may discover vast crowds of these tiny, transparent animals, just below the surface of an outdoor water-tank – or buy some from an aquarium shop. Examine a water-flea in a drop of water on a glass slide, under a low-power microscope. You will be thrilled to see its little heart beating.

water-flea in water drop –enlarged many times

Caddis-fly larvae

caddis-fly larva in case

caddis-fly

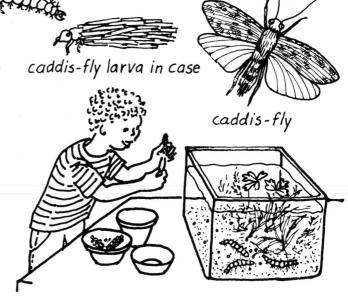

You will recognize these underwater larvae because they live inside tubes, which they build from sand grains, bits of shell or plant debris. Gently remove some caddis-fly larvae from their tubes, using tweezers. Put the naked larvae in an aquarium with some sand mixed with minute, colored beads – and see how they will build the materials into new tubes. The adult is a moth-like fly, active by night. Release the larvae into a pond or stream, after your experiment.

Dragonfly nymph

dragonfly nymph attacking

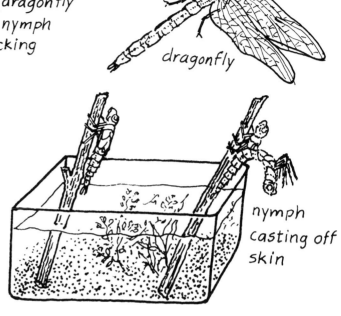

dragonfly

This is a vicious underwater monster, with an underlip device called a mask – pincer-like jaws that can be pushed out to grab a tadpole or young fish. Keep one for a few days' observation. If you are greatly interested, you could wait patiently, to see if it will climb up a stick, out of the water, to become a beautiful dragonfly. Dragonflies cannot sting any animal – but they are agile as insect helicopters, doing useful work by hawking for midges, mosquitoes and even wasps.

nymph casting off skin

Can you get a frog to hibernate?

During the winter frogs hide in mud under ponds, not feeding and breathing very slowly through their skins, until warmer weather and a plentiful food supply arrive. Prepare a special aquarium, with a mud bank at one end. Cover, to stop the frog escaping. Put it in a cool place for some hours, then float ice cubes in the water and put some on the bank. Watch the frog's breathing getting slower, as the animal gets sluggish and starts to dig itself into the watery mud. Then let it warm up gradually – and let it go.

Wild creatures near your home

cat

dog

fox

Looking for evidence of mammals

Are there foxes in your neighborhood? There is ample evidence that foxes are living in and around towns. They even breed in people's gardens. Check out any local reports of fox sitings. Can you identify the rather pointed tracks of a fox in the snow?

Molehills in gardens will tell you that moles are about, although you will be lucky to actually see one. Hedgehogs are regularly killed on roads. They are mesmerized by car lights. If you suspect that there is a hedgehog visiting your garden (little-finger-sized black droppings on your lawn) you might put out a saucer of bread and milk for it.

Unfortunately, a dead animal on the road is the most usual sign that mammals are about. Most of them are more active by night. But you will see squirrels by day in towns. Perhaps you have some living nearby. They raid bird-feeders. Try to catch sight of one eating berries, gripping on to the branches of a tree with its hind legs. A grey squirrel knows how to pull up an apple core that is hanging on a string from a branch.

water-vole

If you have a stream by your house, you might catch a day-time glimpse of a water-vole (*not* a rat) swimming in the water. Other mammals to look for near your home are fieldmice, bats and – dare I mention them – rats. Badgers sometimes live in the suburbs. I have seen a grey house mouse, in broad daylight, running along the sidewalk on Seventh Avenue, New York.

A page from a nature notebook

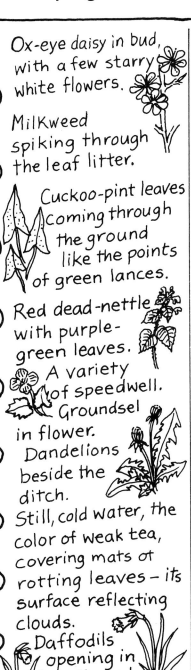

Ox-eye daisy in bud, with a few starry white flowers.

Milkweed spiking through the leaf litter.

Cuckoo-pint leaves coming through the ground like the points of green lances.

Red dead-nettle with purple-green leaves. A variety of speedwell. Groundsel in flower. Dandelions beside the ditch.

Still, cold water, the color of weak tea, covering mats of rotting leaves – its surface reflecting clouds. Daffodils opening in sheltered places.

Bramble leaves in the wood– still green after the winter, purple-edged and riddled with the winding passages of leaf-mining insect larvae.

A mad-sounding cry, weaker than the green woodpecker's, and the sound of a tree being pecked – then, just ahead, a lesser-spotted woodpecker, black and white barred, fluffy plumage. It stayed about 5 seconds before taking flight noisily. From a narrow field with oak trees in the hedgerows, the sound of mewing. A commotion of departing wood pigeons.

Then the gliding form of a buzzard.

A flock of seagulls, soaring round and round, very high in a rising warm bubble of air, drifting westward, in a grey wintry sky.

J. was impressed last year, when we watched hawks ascending in this way– 'screwing rain out of the sky' as country people say. J. said he wouldn't forget that. sparrows rebuilding nests at Smithtown Sanctuary. Some birds apparently stealing sticks from an occupied nest. (Observations in the week ending 10th March 1984)

Keep a notebook of your nature observations. It will encourage you to look at your surroundings more attentively. If you are interested in writing, such a notebook is a useful way to give yourself regular practice.

Sky-watching

Some of the most beautiful scenery is in the sky. When the world at ground level looks drab and dull, a glance at the sky may reveal changing cloudscapes that suggest mountains, lakes and islands. And, looking up, you may see the moon by day and swifts performing rapid aerobatics around the buildings in a city. Vast swarms of starlings coming to roost on high ledges in towns have an awesome, magical appearance. To a distant observer, their clearly shaped formations sub-divide, re-form and change.

Star-gazing

Can you recognize the star-group called The Big Dipper, with its two "pointers" that show the way to a somewhat pale Pole Star? This star is roughly over the North Pole, so it gives a reliable impression of which direction is North. In day-time, if you have an idea of the time, you can get a useful sense of direction if you remember that the sun, which rises in the East, is South at mid-day, after which it seems to move towards the West.

The word DOC tells you whether the phases of the moon are waxing (getting bigger) or waning (getting smaller). If the shape of the moon resembles a D it is waxing. At full moon the shape is an O. Then a C-shaped moon must be waning. Look at the moon through powerful binoculars. You should just be able to make out the moon's mountains. On a night when a lunar eclipse occurs, you will see the curved edge of the earth's shadow crossing the moonscape.

Make a habit of sky-watching, but also look where you go.

Clouds and weather

Clouds form when invisible water vapor (gas) condenses into tiny drops of water that float in the sky, like mist. Watch the vapor from your breath condense on a cold window – or make a "cloud" on a frosty day. The sun's heat makes water evaporate. The vapor rises with warmed air into regions where the pressure of the atmosphere is less – and so the air can expand. Expanding cools the air. (Use an aerosol. Feel the nozzle afterwards. Lowering the pressure of the gas inside makes the can feel cool.) Water vapor from cooling air condenses to form clouds.

The four main types of clouds are fluffy cumulus, high, icy wisps of hair-like cirrus, grey layers of stratus and dark nimbus. Cumulus occur in fine weather, but they mean thunderstorms if they pile up high in the sky and darken on top. Cirrus clouds denote a coming change in the weather. Stratus clouds, especially if they darken to nimbus, mean rain. When the fine mist particles in clouds get larger, they fall as rain – or as snow if the temperature is low enough. Raindrops falling through very cold air may freeze to form hailstones. Mists and denser mists called fog are clouds on the ground.

Water vapor in the air is called humidity. Warm air can hold more vapor than cold air. This helps to explain why water vapor in the air condenses when the air gets cooler. Air that is holding as much water vapor as it can at a particular temperature is saturated. Humid air is so nearly saturated that sweat cannot evaporate properly and we feel uncomfortable. When the temperature of the air falls below its saturation point by night, water vapor condenses on the ground as dew, to form frost if it freezes. Look for golden reflections of the sun in dew-drops and for frost patterns on spiders' webs.

Can you tell weather?

Weather arrives with the winds. South and West winds bring fine weather as a rule, but expect a change when they become gusty. Northerly winds bring wintry weather. Easterlies bring wet, cold weather in the winter and spring months, but they arrive with hot spells for the summer. A barometer provides reliable clues about what weather you can expect. When it shows that the air pressure is gradually rising, look forward to fine weather, but do not go out without your raincoat if the pressure is falling.

A lurid red glow under clouds is a rain sign, but a rosy-red sky at nightfall means that fine weather is likely the next day. Pale yellow sky means that rain and wind will follow, and rain will fall very soon from a sky colored with a greenish tint. Morning mist after one hot day is generally followed by another scorcher.

Check out these weather signs from folklore, to see if they are reliable: Rain can be expected if you notice spiders deserting their webs, if farm animals shelter from the wind, if earthworms are active on the surface by day, if dust swirls in the wind, or if smells from flowers are more noticeable. Catching sight of a black "rain beetle" or getting an unusually clear view of distant hills are also rain signs. Swifts and swallows flying high, owls hooting gently at dusk and a cock crowing in a rainstorm are supposed to forecast fine weather.

Keep a piece of seaweed hanging up outside. It gets damp when rain is approaching. Rain is also due, when people complain that their corns ache and throb.

seaweed

Snow crystals

How many varieties of snow can you recognize? The English language has few words to describe them, but observant Eskimos have more than 20 words for different kinds of snow. Although a snow blanket is freezing on top, the temperature at ground level may be as much as 45°F warmer – thus protecting plants from the effects of frost. Air trapped amongst the snow is a poor conductor of heat from the soil.

Snowflakes are like people – no two are ever exactly alike. Examine them out-of-doors, just after they fall on your sleeve. Use a magnifying-glass. You should be able to see the typical snow crystal pattern – like 6-pointed stars.

Fold squares of thin white paper as the pictures show, then cut them as suggested, to make snowflake patterns when they are opened out. To get different shapes, vary the rough outlines of the points. But always cut one point longer than the other, to make a more realistic snowflake shape. Decorate for Christmas with a paper snowstorm.

1 fold square of paper in half

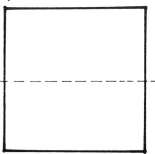

2 mark center

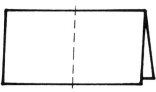

3 mark 60° angle

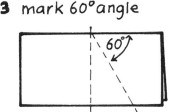

4 fold right side down at 60° angle

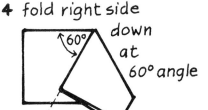

5 fold left side across at 60°

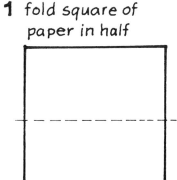

6 mark center

7 fold left side across right

8 cut

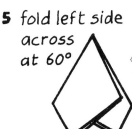

47

Index